POEMS

FOR

8

YEAR OLDS

POEMS
FOR
8
YEAR OLDS

MATT GOODFELLOW

ILLUSTRATED BY ROXANA DE ROND

MACMILLAN CHILDREN'S BOOKS

Published 2022 by Macmillan Children's Books
an imprint of Pan Macmillan
The Smithson, 6 Briset Street, London EC1M 5NR
EU representative: Macmillan Publishers Ireland Ltd, 1st Floor,
The Liffey Trust Centre, 117–126 Sheriff Street Upper
Dublin 1, D01 YC43
Associated companies throughout the world
www.panmacmillan.com

ISBN 978-1-5290-6530-5

1 3 5 7 9 8 6 4 2

A CIP catalogue record for this book is available from the British Library.

Printed and bound by CPI Group (UK) Ltd, Croydon CR0 4YY

To my grandpa, Norman Goodfellow –
you are loved and missed x

CONTENTS

READY, STEADY, READ!

A Performance Poem About Reading

Here's a book . . .
       GET SET   **Pick!**
Shall I lift it like a weight?
Or aim it like a stick?

I could jump or I could juggle
– it might end up as a muddle
What to do?
I haven't a clue . . .

I could perch it on my head and walk straight and TALL
How long can I do that before it takes a fall?
. . . oh . . . not very long at all . . .

What *can* I do with a book?
Jump with it?
Swim with it?
Hop with it?
Win with it
Or . . .
Open up the book
                 . . . And take a look . . .
Ah . . . on my marks . . . dive in!

Michaela Morgan

FREE

and we will open all the doors

and we will jump on all the beds

and we will leap from mountain top to mountain top

and we will laugh until we think we might explode

and we will laugh especially in those moments when we
    aren't really supposed to

and we will of course find this only makes the laughing
    a million times more extreme

and we will talk to animals

and we will stride across oceans

and we will dance like maniacs

and we will lie on the sofa watching TV with our shoes
    on because why not

and we will have long baths/short baths/no baths delete
    as applicable

and we will eat delicious foods

and we will not eat any of the bits we don't really like

and we will talk while lying on our backs and looking at
    the sky

and we will say the first thing that pops into our heads

and we will be always with our friends even when we
    are not

and we will smile with smiles so deep they make our
    eyes disappear
and we will grow wings
and we will
and we will
and we will

Kate Wakeling

ME

When I was three, was I really me,
The me that I am right now?
And when I was four, was I more than before?
Did that me grow inside me? And how?
Then when I turned five, was the me yet alive,
The me that I am now I'm eight?
Did that me just appear with the change of a year,
Or did it sit lying in wait?
And the me that I'll be when I'm *seventy*-three –
Does it exist, in a way?
Or perhaps my me changes, through all my life's ranges,
Each month, or each week, or each day?
Does the me with my name remain always the same,
Is there anything there that can last?
Or is it unreal, this me that I feel?
Oh these questions are simply too vast!

Elli Woollard

I HAVE ALWAYS KNOWN

I have always known
That at last I would
Take this road, but yesterday
I did not know that it would be today.

Narihara
(translated by Kenneth Rexroth)

WiNDOW

Through my window
I can see
a bird on a branch
in a ragged tree.

A thin rain falls
from the great, grey sky
and the small bird sings
so shrill and high.

A faint breeze blows
some blossom down.
The petals are pink
and the earth is brown.

It feels like the world
lies under a spell,
this world I know
and love so well.

I'm at the window.
The bird's in the tree.
And life goes on
mysteriously.

Tony Mitton

EARSTORM

snow and rain and
slush and snizzle
snail and slosh and
whooshes
slice slithering
shice snivelling
shunt shooting
shilly shally splattering
ICE
ice hey!
I say!
supersounds
snot jussnice
sloverly

Jan Dean

TO THE BEARS

I've gone to the bears.
To the woods,
to the rivers,
to the black caves.
I've gone to be brave.
I've gone where the
big bears roam.
I won't miss school
or my old home.
I'll be with the bears.
I'll go where they go.
I'll tramp with them
through the deep snow.
I'll growl if they do.
I'll roar if I want to.
I've gone to the bears.
I've gone where the
dark streams leap
with the wild fish.
Where stars shine bright
on a child's wish.

I'll shake the trees
till the leaves fall.
I'll stamp my foot
like a bear's paw. I'll
eat honey like the bears do.
Do you want to come too?

Louise Greig

A SONG OF TOAD

The world has held great Heroes,
As history-books have showed;
But never a name to go down to fame
Compared with that of Toad!

The clever men at Oxford
Know all that there is to be knowed.
But they none of them knew one half as much
As intelligent Mr Toad!

The animals sat in the Ark and cried,
Their tears in torrents flowed.
Who was it said, 'There's land ahead'?
Encouraging Mr Toad!

The Army all saluted
As they marched along the road.
Was it the King? Or Kitchener?
No. It was Mr Toad!

The Queen and her ladies-in-waiting
Sat at the window and sewed.
She cried, 'Look! who's that *handsome* man?'
They answered, 'Mr Toad.'

The motor-car went Poop-poop-poop
As it raced along the road.
Who was it steered it into a pond?
Ingenious Mr Toad!

Kenneth Grahame

NAMESAKE

Catch me in a bird's song.
See me in the stars.
Rest with me on the seashore
to the turning tide's applause.
Find me in a flower.
Hold me in your heart.
Walk with me in a garden.
Look for me in art.
Taste me in a cup of tea
of all unlikely places.
See me shine through wrinkles
in kind old faces.
I am a lamb beside its mother
nestling in her fleece.
Smell me in my namesake rose,
pick me, I am *Peace*.

Celia Warren

Transition Day

I don't know how the teachers decide
who to keep together, who to divide

but my friend Noah went into Class Four
while I was sent through a different door.

Felt sad all day. Though my new teacher's cool,
next term I won't want to go to school.

I'll just wait all morning till it's time to play
and count the days till Saturday,

I'll cross off the weeks for term to end
and Noah will always be my best friend.

Carole Bromley

MEAN WORDS

Words. I hold on to them.
Something someone says
– just a little thing,
just a 'BY-THE-WAY'.
It's not meant to stay
But it does.

I hold on tight, you see.
Scrunch it in my hands,
stuff it under my pillow,
think about it all night.
I don't mean to
But I do.

Then sometimes I think
what if
I just
let go?
What then?

What if I choose
the words to keep,
(the kind ones),
the words to chuck
(the rest)?

What if *I* have the power?
What then?

Then I'd sleep.
Then I'd wake up.
Then I'd be free.

Rashmi Sirdeshpande

MOTHER TONGUE

Cloud is not my first language
I understand a few words
their greeting for morning
three silent names for a storm
those for light and air
eight words for sky
I have tried to write
but how to spell them

I cannot speak stone, ancient
igneous, always changed
its rune-words half fossil
guttural and glacial
all rough consonants
five words for cracks
eight for avalanche
and as for mountain . . .

Naturally I'm fluent
in tree, ponderous creatures
ah but they don't say much
when they do it's a whisper
one word for root
for everything
it's just percussion
without the diction

And who ever knew water
mostly it just babbles, fish
speak some and pebbles
you think you understand
then it bursts banks
or just dries up
and then when it rains
no punctuation

Sue Hardy-Dawson

LAVENDER'S BLUE

Lavender's blue, dilly dilly, lavender's green,
When I am king, dilly dilly, you shall be queen.
Who told you so, dilly dilly, who told you so?
'Twas mine own heart, dilly dilly, that told me so.

Call up your men, dilly dilly, set them to work,
Some with a rake, dilly dilly, some with a fork,
Some to make hay, dilly dilly, some to thresh corn,
Whilst you and I, dilly dilly, keep ourselves warm.

Anon.

DiARY OF A GHOST

Monday
    Bad day.
    Died.
    Accident with yogurt maker.

Tuesday
    Buried.
    People cried,
    But not me,
    Cos I chose
    To be a GHOST!

Wednesday
    Rose from the dead.
    For some reason,
    It hurts your chin.
    Practised wailing,
    Floating,
    And walking through walls.

Thursday
   Haunted my sister.
   She had headphones on –
   Never even noticed!
   She's still annoying me
   Beyond the grave.

Friday
   Spooked some lads
   Playing footie
   Behind the school.
   Ha, ha, ha,
   That was good.

Saturday
 Had a day off today.
 Went to Leeds.
 I miss food.
 Ghosts don't eat,
 You see.

Sunday
 Bored.
 Haunting is hard work.
 And, well,
 I don't have any friends.
 Leeds was all right.

Monday
 I've been dead a week.
 It's funny what you miss.
 Socks,
 The feel of grass,
 Stroking the cat.
 It's hard to say, but
 I don't want to be
 A ghost
 Any more.

Andy Seed

BLOODY SAMOSAS

(for Halloween or any scary event)

Take a shiny silver knife
to a ready-to-eat shaking samosa
chop it in half, better still
using bare hands – tear it apart
lay out its parts flat and splatter
with blood red ketchup
or smoking hot chilli sauce
repeat until you have
a massacre of slaughtered
samosas. Eat the bloody samosas.
Like an Indian vampire
shaking your head side to side
saying – yes – yummy – yes
when finished – all gone.
Put your hands up and
surrender – admitting
Yes I am the samosa murderer
But you can't prove it
Because I've eaten
All the evidence. Ha.

Anjum Malik

MY HALLOWEEN PARTY

I hosted a party one dark Halloween,
My guests were aghast when a ghost could be seen
Descending the stairs looking lanky and lean,
With nothing up there where his head had once been.

They told me they thought me a horrible host,
And mine was the household they hated the most.
Of course, I feel guilty, but cannot help boast:
A party goes best if you've got a good ghost!

Colin West

MY NAME

Grandma says she knows my name
(And my picture's in her photo frame),
Sometimes my name is just mislaid
Like glasses, pens, or hearing aid.

Sometimes, she searches for a while,
Touches my lips, traces my smile,
Then tells a tale I've heard before
About a party dress she wore.

Sometimes she thinks I'm someone else,
Dad says, 'Now, don't upset yourself,'
And in her eyes I see the spaces
She tries to fill with familiar faces.

Her memories have gathered dust,
She doesn't quite know who to trust,
Some days she stares, some days she cries,
And when she does, I wipe her eyes.

Grandma says she knows my name,
Just not at the moment when I came
To see her, but she hasn't lied,
I know my name is locked inside.

Coral Rumble

I SAW A SHIP A-SAILING

I saw a ship a-sailing
A-sailing on the sea
And oh but it was laden
With lovely things for me

There were chocolates in the cabin
And ice cream in the hold
The sails were made of candyfloss
And the masts were all of gold

The four-and-twenty sailors
That stood between the decks
Were four-and-twenty white mice
With ribbons round their necks

The captain was a duck
With a parrot on his back
And when the mice were naughty
The captain said, 'Quack! Quack!'

Anon.

CHAFFINCH

One mother bird keeps
five marbled eggs warm

sings to them quietly
until they are born

nestled in cobwebs
and moss in her nest

five baby birds snug
in her feathered breast

deep in the holly
her five nestling brood

have little beaks open
all chirping for food

five feathered chaff-chicks
flap wings, learn to fly

till one day wind takes them
free as song and sky

Liz Brownlee

TRANSCRiPTiON OF A NiGHTiNGALE'S SONG

chew chew chee chew chee
chew – cheer cheer cheer
chew chew chew chee
– up cheer up cheer up
tweet tweet tweet jug jug jug

wew wew wew – chur chur
woo it woo it tweet tweet
tweet jug jug jug

tee rew tee rew tee rew – gur
gur – chew rit chew rit – chur-chur chur
chur will-will will-will tweet-em
tweet em jug jug jug jug

grig grig grig chew chew

wevy wit wevy wit
wevy wit – chee-chit
chee-chit chee chit
weewit weewit wee
wit cheer cheer
cheer – pelew
pelew pelew –
bring a jug bring a
jug bring a jug

John Clare

THINGS THAT SHOULD BE IN A POEM

The sleep in my eyes,
The wax in my ears,
The salt on my cheek
From stray night-time tears,

The squeeze of my jumper,
The swish of my hair,
The crack in my curtain,
The dust in the air,

My skip on the pavement,
My jump from the wall,
The gathering treasure
As large conkers fall,

The squelch of my boots,
The mud in their grooves,
The wobble of puddles
Before they go smooth,

A weekend of time,
A wide space to play,
I think I'll collect
A poem today.

Coral Rumble

HALF TERM

'It'll burn off,' Mum says as autumn mist blurs the world
The cold smack of morning rosies my cheeks
and chases the sleep from my eyes
covering my bed-ruffled hair with glittering dewy beads
I pull my cold wellies on to my warm and bare feet
and my jacket over my pyjamas
whispering excitement into the quiet of early morning
Dad already has that faraway look in his eyes.
He has the memory of sharp heather-scent in his lungs
and the silence of the hills in his thoughts
the salt of the sea in his beard
Mum carries my sleeping sister to the car
and slides her in on top of the blankets
and clothes
and toys
and books
and the folded canvas of a tent that still smells of last
    year's storm
I wriggle in and make a nest in the back seat
'Look,' Mum says as she tucks the blanket around us
and straps us safely in for the long drive,
'camping weather!'

Dawn McLachlan

A Plea From the Rescue Centre for Mythical Beasts

One or two of our mythical creatures
have proved very hard to rehome.
Nobody wants a gorgon
whose stare could turn them to stone.

But a dragon below the floorboards
will provide you with underfloor heating.
Many heads of a hydra will watch
from each window while you're sleeping.

Roars from a centaur will help
keep away burglars too.
And a Cyclops will always say
that he's keeping his eye on you.

A banshee's high-pitched shriek
will wake you from your sleep,
better than any alarm clock
if your sleep is heavy and deep.

Cerberus, the three-headed dog,
will cause a stir in the park,
warning off rival dogs
with his fearsome bark, bark, bark.

Some creatures we can't get enough of,
like the popular unicorn,
and everyone wants to rehome
a lucky leprechaun.

An ogre for classroom discipline
would be of assistance to teachers.
So won't you help us rehome
one of our mythical creatures?

Brian Moses

WHAT iS PiNK?

What is pink? A rose is pink
By the fountain's brink.
What is red? A poppy's red
In its barley bed.
What is blue? The sky is blue
Where the clouds float through.
What is white? A swan is white
Sailing in the light.
What is yellow? Pears are yellow,
Rich and ripe and mellow.
What is green? The grass is green,
With small flowers between.
What is violet? Clouds are violet
In the summer twilight.
What is orange? Why, an orange,
Just an orange!

Christina Rossetti

52 BLUE – THE LONELiEST WHALE

He's a high-pitched singer
crystal ringer
dancing on his own
like a lone gunslinger
firing out beats
of water notation
spinning his song
in his own rotation.

Big and wide
rocking side to side
taking his groove
out for a ride
in a musical ocean
lending the notion
swimming the depths
in a blissed-out motion

He's a mover a groover
a big shrimp hoover
chewing out tunes
guaranteed to move her
setting the pace
to a lumbering grace
always a sun-happy
smile on his face.

52 Blue.
Unique not new.
Dancing to the word
that can't be heard.
52 Blue
52 Blue
Dancing for himself
Not me or you.

Dom Conlon

52 Blue is the name of a single whale who sings at a higher frequency than any other whale on earth. That means none of the other whales can hear the song and so never reply.

SiLVER SANDALS

when I wear my silver sandals   I'm who I want to be
walking forward   head held high   no one's
               stopping me

when I wear my silver sandals   all the hard words
      go away
shadow-spaces fill with light no matter what they say

when I wear my silver sandals   I give in to no demands
everyone that sees me knows and understands

this girl in silver sandals holds the world within her
hands

Matt Goodfellow

FiSH

Fish dart
together, part
fish gleam
roll and laze
quicksilver blaze
fish stream

fish flight
in swimming light
fish beam
dot and dash
needle-flash
fish seam

fish drowse
bubble-browse
fish teem
shallow, deep
shadowed sleep
fish dream

Imogen Russell Williams

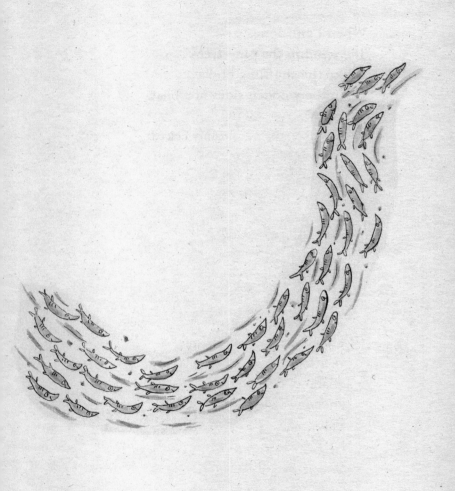

THE FiSHERMAN'S WiFE

When I am alone,
The wind in the pine-trees
Is like the shuffling of waves
Upon the wooden sides of a boat.

Amy Lowell

BEACH PEBBLE

she feels
cold water creep
beneath her belly before
the soft white foam
draws her
inside

.

she is
the shifting shingle
below wrinkled waves
she is the sigh of ocean's breath
gentled and rounded
then placed to dry
under a salted
sun

.

one
million tides
may fold and form
one billion pebbles
but she whispers
her own
story

John Rice

SOMEWHERE out there is that hare.
   Has to be. Saw it last week. Just over
the road, beyond the barn, amidst the gold

of the corn field. Thought it was a rabbit;
   then we clocked those ears, and whoa,
did that flatfoot go. So swift! Across

the land with a leap and a bound,
   like its cousin could only dream of.
So we'll wait till late to head out there,

to glimpse that whiskery whizz of a hare,
   that non-stop nomad, dweller-of-nowhere –
but absolutely *anywhere* . . .

James Carter

INFANT INNOCENCE

The grizzly bear is huge and wild;
He has devoured the infant child.
The infant child is not aware
He has been eaten by the bear.

A. E. Housman

POCKETS

Her pockets are never empty.
She says pockets are for running.
So she keeps them full,
Stuffs universes into them,
And says it is just the essentials.

She says: if we get stranded,
If aliens take us,
If there's an apocalypse,
There will be no time for bags.

She treats pockets
Like built-in spaces for hope.
Lets the weight of it
Pull down her baggy trousers.

Readies herself for any eventuality,
Revels in her own lack of normality.

Ruth Awolola

WORD HOARD

Long ago,
when people laid straw on their floors,
and played football with pigs' bladders
and stuck leeches on the legs of the sick,
long *long* ago —
well, they made word hoards.

A word hoard is a set of words
with a certain magic about them.
They're words that stir the spirit
and tingle on the tongue.

A word hoard is a secret stash of vocab
that makes your heart hum.

Now, you might like a word
for its sound
or for its sense.

Or you might like a word
for both its music *and* its meaning,
like . . . *picnic* perhaps?

In any case,
what you put in your word hoard
is up to you.

Here's mine:

quick	*tendril*	*magic*	*feast*
root	*music*	*weird*	*fierce*
thirst	*blossom*	*curse*	*drift*
bright	*worm*	*wander*	*sleep*

What words,
I wonder,
might you keep
in yours?

Kate Wakeling

THE WAY THROUGH THE WOODS

They shut the road through the woods
Seventy years ago.
Weather and rain have undone it again,
And now you would never know
There was once a road through the woods
Before they planted the trees.
It is underneath the coppice and heath,
And the thin anemones.
Only the keeper sees
That, where the ring-dove broods,
And the badgers roll at ease,
There was once a road through the woods.

Yet, if you enter the woods
Of a summer evening late,
When the night-air cools on the trout-ringed pools
Where the otter whistles his mate,
(They fear not men in the woods,
Because they see so few.)
You will hear the beat of a horse's feet,
And the swish of a skirt in the dew,
Steadily cantering through
The misty solitudes,
As though they perfectly knew
The old lost road through the woods.
But there is no road through the woods.

Rudyard Kipling

FELiCiTY

Felicity bullies
Felicity's fierce
Her eyes when she glares
Are lasers that pierce.
Felicity pinches
And jabs with her comb

Felicity dawdles
On her way home.

Philip Waddell

A Short List of Alternatives

Climb à tree
Or drink some tea
Or spend some time
With your family

Write a song
Or sing along
To your favourite popstars'
Newest songs

Make memes and laugh away
Or watch films or write a play
Or leave your pajamas on and stay
Indoors reading all day today.

Go for a walk
Or have a heartfelt talk
Or paint a rock
Or knit some socks.

I could go on
But I'm running out of room
Yet I think you get
What I'm trying to say

There's a thousand
Better things to do today
Instead of being mean or sending hate
Someone else's way.

Nikita Gill

MY TALENTED TALKING TOE

It doesn't matter where I go,
or how I travel – fast or slow,
though neither of my parents know,
        I have a talented talking toe.

He chitter chatters day and night,
he sometimes tries to pick a fight
with other toes, or cause a fright.
He really could be more polite,
        my teeny tempestuous toe.

He's grumpy when I put on shoes
cause then he cannot share his news
or tell me of his tawdry views –
I'd walk barefoot if toe could choose.
I sometimes wish he'd take a snooze,
        my tiresome tenacious toe.

Although my toe is often boring,
Toe is really reassuring,
Toe gives me a steady mooring,
so, in fact, I'm quite adoring
of my brave and bold, exploring,
talking, singing and guffawing
        toe-tally tip top toe.

Laura Mucha

BAKE SALE

Chocolatey cornflakes and coconut ice,
fruity Dundee cake and hot apple pies,
cool-bags of kulfi, Victoria sponge,
baklava, bundt cakes and fat currant buns,
lemony madeleines, light panettone,
treacly parkin and creamy cannoli,
beautiful mooncakes and apricot malva,
lamingtons, gingerbread, crumbling halva,
shattering chikki and rich bara brith,
brownies and buttery rugelach twists,
Black Forest gateau and candied cassata,
kipferl and strudel and fragrant gizzada,
chequerboard Battenberg, cobbler with peach:
I couldn't decide so I bought some of each.

Rachel Piercey

FLYiNG HORSE iN THE MOONLiGHT

Two nights ago a horse flew over our house.
Luckily for me the push-button moon was full
so I could make out the reddish-yellow markings
on the flying horse's flanks and see clearly
his branch-brown belly.

He had a tight-closed mouth and his wise eyes
made him look so aloof, so superior.
His mane and tail were trailing in what little wind
there was. With every stride his body curved, straightened
and arched; curved, straightened and arched –
a night-dark swimmer.

As he steeplechased over our house, right above me,
I felt a rush of dry, warm air brush my face.
It made me close my eyes for a second, but lightly.
All around everything was glazed pale in the moonlight –
the trees, the houses, the gardens, the pavements –
only the horse showed his true, earthly colours.

I called out to him. Not words, just a stifled cry.
But I don't suppose he heard me
for he galloped on without looking back.
I think some birds were following him,
but they were dark and small. They flew so fast
I couldn't make them out. Might have been starlings.

Of course no one believed me
when I told them about the flying horse,
but next time there's a full moon, I'll stay up
all night to watch for him, again.

John Rice

MEDICAL ROOM

If you run into a tree
And you slightly graze your knee —

Wet Paper Towel!

If your nose begins to bleed
Or your private parts get kneed —

Wet Paper Towel!

If you've come out in a rash
Or you think you've got whiplash —

Wet Paper Towel!

If you've fallen in the mud
Or an artery's spurting blood —

Wet Paper Towel!

If you've got a nasty cough
Or your left leg's fallen off —

Wet Paper Towel!

If your symptoms are quite vague
Or you may have caught the plague –

Wet Paper Towel!

If a bully's on the prowl
Or you've just been disembowelled –

Wet Paper Towel!
Wet Paper Towel!
Wet Paper Towel!

Sarah Ziman

YANKEE DOODLE

Yankee Doodle went to town,
He rode a little pony,
He stuck a feather in his hat
And called it macaroni.

Yankee Doodle fa, so, la,
Yankee Doodle dandy.
Yankee Doodle fa, so, la,
Buttermilk and brandy,

Yankee Doodle went to town
To buy a pair of trousers,
He swore he could not see the town
For so many houses.

Yankee Doodle fa, so, la,
Yankee Doodle dandy.
Yankee Doodle fa, so, la,
Buttermilk and brandy.

Anon.

JUST WHO DO YOU THINK YOU ARE?

after Tomaž Šalamun

I am the original whizz-kid.
I am chocolate biscuits, I am cherry ice cream,
I am Christmas. I am someone else's turn to do the dishes.
I am the last day of school, I am helium balloons,
I am cruising downstream, the sun's signature tune.
I am making up limericks, I am possessed of great magic
    tricks,
I am homemade chips with ketchup, I am.

In harmony with all creation you have to admit
that I am a ride-on lawnmower; the grass pays homage
    to me,
the alphabet spaghetti makes words for me every day.
I am just everything — strawberries in winter,
the all-you-can-eat hamburger van. I am bop till you drop,
I am without *stop* or *do not*.

I have no cringey clothes, no back-bending knees.
I am the A-star, I am first for the bathwater.
Behold my mud-splattered snapped-elastic socks!
Behold me rip through the cereal box for the plastic gift!

The carrot cake is amazed, the lemonade is waving.
Who is the chief of pizza?
I am the birthday feast
that no flat fizz can ever let down.

I am the relief of cool lotion on an insect bite.
I am the afternoon of non-stop cartoons.
I am the all-new anti-nightmare device,
I hold back the forces of gloom and fright.
Beside me, every bright spark grows dim.
Beside me, every neon light seems dark.

I'm every secret. Every rocket. Every party. Every tune.
Every low-down. Every showdown. Every rainbow and
    typhoon.
Every drop-kick. Every hat-trick. Every cat-that-got-the-
    cream.
Every kid stuck on the sidelines, still not picked for any
    team.

Shauna Darling Robertson

ADVICE

Suck it up,
Buttercup.
Reach for socks —
pull them up.
Bite the bullet.
Don't say die.
Seize the day.
Learn to fly.
Pay the piper.
Take the rap.
Pay attention.
Mind the

gap.

Kate O'Neil

THERE WAS A YOUNG MAIDEN CALLED MAGGIE

There was a small maiden named Maggie,
Whose dog was enormous and shaggy;
The front end of him
Looked vicious and grim –
But the tail end was friendly and waggy.

Anon.

BLACK BEAR BACKS UP TO THE GIANT PINE TREE

Itches dart, quick as fish
beneath her rippling coat.
Itch, fish, scratch.

Black bear backs up
to the giant pine tree.
Red, bark, rough.

Her heart slows
as she starts to scrub.
Dub-dub, dub-dub, dub-dub.

Birds are alarmed
as branches sway.
Flap, sky, up.

Rattling pine cones
come raining down.
Ground, bounce, thump.

Black bear is done,
the fish are gone.
Giant, joy, rub.

Mandy Coe

DON'T BE LATE

At the edge of the park we dawdle by the bridge, waiting
talked out
All games played
All things said
Long summer day rolled over into evening blue
We wait until the very last moment.
The 'tink' of streetlights blinking on
our starter pistol
and we run
Scattering the dry grass with our fast feet
The cold breath of oncoming night tugs at us
but we are too fast for it
Nothing can catch us
We are as fleet as the wind
Dividing wordless at our own streets
we lose sight of each other in the creep of the dark
and fly like moths towards the light of our doorsteps
Bursting in
the night air pours off us
Wrapped in the bright warmth of the threshold
We call out
'We're home!'

Dawn McLachlan

WiLD WiLD GiRL

Today I found a wild wild girl
she lives down by the river.
She caught a trout with her bare hands,
I watched it flip and quiver!
She sparked a fire with flints
so we cooked the fish for tea;
she kept the bones for soup
then scrambled up a tree;
faster than a lynx, clever as a bear,
she waved to me to join her
in the green and dappled air.
As I climbed up, branch to branch,
so quick and keen and free,
I sang out to the forest
'This wild wild girl is me!'

Sophie Kirtley

BEE BUDDiES

Two giddy school children
on a broken yellow bike
one reading from the wings
of an upside-down map
whilst the other
steers from the knees

neither know their
left from their right
yet both are certain
they'll be friends for life
that their destination
will appear somewhere

as they hum
the half-remembered tune
their grandmothers sang
lying top-to-toe in the field
with buttery suns nodding
at the pathlessness of days.

Dom Conlon

WY iS SCHOOL A FiNG

wy is school a fing
it is inoing and it is boring
and the teachers are enoing
work is boring
wy is school a thing
reading is trash
we haf to do crap poims at school
ther is no xbox
why is school a thing

Sonny (aged 8)

REQUIEM

Under the wide and starry sky
Dig the grave and let me lie:
Glad did I live and gladly die,
And I laid me down with a will.

This be the verse you grave for me:
Here he lies where he longed to be;
Home is the sailor, home from sea,
And the hunter home from the hill.

Robert Louis Stevenson

IF YOU'VE EVER SEEN A WOLF

in the wild — or so the old
saying goes — it's seen you

a thousand times before.
So maybe the same is true
of a mouse. Think of whenever

you've been alone and made
the most of that moment:
you've sung so loud; invented

a dance; bounced on your bed
like a kangaroo. And once, just
once — you may have discovered

that you had been watched
by a mouse: apricot-brown,
with two unblinking, ebony eyes.

So what to do? Nothing.
Be good to your whiskery
neighbour: it will not judge,

nor laugh at you, nor grade
    your dance out of 5. Just let
it return to the world below,

knowing your home
    is no longer
your own.

James Carter
for National Poetry Day 2020

Letters from the Lost

We are the lost things
from where lost things go
kites plucked from oaks
faded by sun
the sad and the worn
those unwanted, forlorn
shades of birthday balloon
on pieces of string

We are the lost things
from where the lost hide
in a mirror's echo
footprints on tides
scattered silver, hairpins
pages torn and thin
the babble of babies
in a soft shoe's sigh

We are the lost things
from where lost things come
the jingle of rings
falling to stones
secrets and wishes
words spoken by rivers
jet, amber and opal
from adder's white skin

We are the lost things
where all lost things are
the damp growl of bear
songs of dead stars
tales no longer told
gloves glittering cold
what you are now
the child that you were . . .

Sue Hardy-Dawson

AUTUMN

In the dreamy silence
Of the afternoon, a
Cloth of gold is woven
Over wood and prairie;
And the jaybird, newly
Fallen from the heaven,
Scatters cordial greetings,
And the air is filled with
Scarlet leaves, that, dropping,
Rise again, as ever,
With a useless sigh for
Rest − and it is Autumn.

Alexander Posey

CONKERS

I was in school.
The day was long.
The evening-fingered night crept on,
touching the streets
closing the park,
the dark.

Mum saved
the warm brown sheen
under the spiky-armoured white and green,
scooped conker cases
into her bag,
knobbly swag.

They lost their lustre soon,
drying to drab –
fat treasures, heel-stomped free
of shell and secrecy.

But Mum's love, that thought of them
that brought them
home to me –

that shone on,
winter, summer,
endlessly.

Imogen Russell Williams

THE WRONG WAY ROUND

sitting
the wrong way round
in the train
can't help but notice
I am heading backwards
through today

cos from my
speeding window-blur
outside fades away
erasing most things
soon minutes vanish
hours dissolve
years hurtle past
then centuries
then ages
world grows younger
and earlier
and earlier

mature trees now saplings
distant mountains shrink to
ancient flat-lands
great whales walk the earth
starlings become packs of
low-swooping dinosaurs

I hurtle backwards
even faster
past last spring
and the winter before that
past my parents
my ancestors
my clan
my species
the rest of living things

until I am an atom
like every other atom
as old and new
as fiery and uncertain
as the fuzzy beginning
of us all

never knowing
let alone dreaming
that one day
I would be me
seated on a train travelling

the wrong way round

Zaro Weil

MAGPiES

One for sorrow
Two for joy
Three for a girl
Four for a boy

Five for silver
Six for gold
Seven for all the joys untold.

Anon.

CRAZE

Everyone had it.
Everyone played with it.
Everyone smuggled it.
Everyone traded it.

I didn't have it.
Wasn't permitted it.
Desperately wanted it.
Couldn't admit to it.

Everyone built on it.
I tried to make it.
Everyone brandished it.
I tried to fake it.

Everyone tired of it
just as I got it.
There was a new it
and my it was not it.

Rachel Piercey

LiSTEN

you can bumble you can bimble on a drum or on a cymbal
you can hey! the ukulele every day
you can bingo on the bongo you can singalingalongo
you can whacka the maraca should you stay

you can pogo on the oboe rola-cola the viola
you can simba the marimba if you please
you can tooty-boot a cutey flute or artichoke a mutey lute
but things that you must never do are these:

never yello at the cello never trickolo the piccolo
or tuck into a snacksaphone for fun
never shaver any quaver bang a mango on the banjo
never mardi-gras an old harmonium

never slammo the piano never Poohstick an acoustic
never lock and steal the glockenspiel my friend
now keep it cool you silly fool there is a final tiny rule
to follow or your little life will end . . .

ALWAYS
ALWAYS
ALWAYS

ignoreder recorder

Matt Goodfellow

THE GRUMPY SHEPHERD

I didn't want to be a shepherd
wearing itchy, purple tights
without any words to say.
At least the lowly ox
got to stand up on a box
in the end of term Christmas play.

I didn't want to be a shepherd
with a tea towel on my head.
Feeling sheepish is not my style.
I should have been the star
shining brightly from afar

and that's why I didn't smile

Rachel Rooney

A SONG iN THE NiGHT

A brown bird sang on a blossomy tree,
   Sang in the moonshine, merrily,
   Three little songs, one, two, and three,
   A song for his wife, for himself, and me.

   He sang for his wife, sang low, sang high,
   Filling the moonlight that filled the sky;
   'Thee, thee, I love thee, heart alive!
   Thee, thee, thee, and thy round eggs five!'

   He sang to himself, 'What shall I do
   With this life that thrills me through and through!
   Glad is so glad that it turns to ache!
   Out with it, song, or my heart will break!'

   He sang to me, 'Man, do not fear
   Though the moon goes down and the dark is near;
   Listen my song and rest thine eyes;
   Let the moon go down that the sun may rise!'

   I folded me up in the heart of his tune,
   And fell asleep with the sinking moon;
   I woke with the day's first golden gleam,
And, lo, I had dreamed a precious dream!

George MacDonald

THE SUPERPOWER SONG

The frosted words to *Auld Lang Syne*
bring sparkle
to a winter midnight

and singing *Happy Birthday*
makes eyes twinkle
and candlelight dance,

but this song explodes
from erupting volcanos.
This song melted the earth's heart.

Sing this song to locked doors and they swing open.
Its tune is as sweet as treacle
and salty as a bag of crisps.

Its words can be sung
in every tongue. It finds
lost ships and steers them home.

This song has rhythm,
this song has rhyme, clocks tick
faster when this song is sung.

Is it a lullaby? Is it an anthem?
Should this song be taught or banned?
Would you lock up birds

who accidentally whistle its tune?
Wait! Who's that singing . . . ?
Is it you? Is it you?

Mandy Coe

QUiNN

My friend Quinn loves ketchup.

It's the *first* thing she thinks of
when a brand-new morning greets her.
I even saw her have ketchup
on tomato-flavoured pizza.
She has it on her corn flakes.
She has it on her curry.
If there's less than half a bottle left,
she really starts to worry.

Her cheeks are covered in ketchup
like a cat's are covered in fur.
My friend Quinn loves ketchup
as much as I love her.

Matt Abbott

WiLD HORSES OF HERGEST RiDGE

There
Through the damp
Cloudy mist
We could just make out
One, two, perhaps three
Grazing on the wet, silk grass of
The Ridge

Rarely seen this far down
Upwards we trudged
Hearts beating
Faster, faster
And oh!
What a sight!

Seven!
White, dapple grey, brown
Breath thick with steam
Serene, silent
Content and unfazed

We stood, we stared,
We whispered
Stared some more
At such a beautiful

Magical, unbelievable sight
Oh! Those wild horses of
Hergest Ridge

Debra Bertulis

Hergest Ridge is a beautiful stretch of common land in Herefordshire,
adjoining England and Wales. Wild horses live here, but catching sight of
them is never guaranteed, as it depends where they're grazing. So, it's always
a wonderful surprise when it happens!

HOME

I came back late and tired last night
    Into my little room,
To the long chair and the firelight
    And comfortable gloom.

But as I entered softly in
    I saw a woman there,
The line of neck and cheek and chin,
    The darkness of her hair,
The form of one I did not know
    Sitting in my chair.

I stood a moment fierce and still,
    Watching her neck and hair.
I made a step to her; and saw
    That there was no one there.

It was some trick of the firelight
    That made me see her there.
It was a chance of shade and light
    And the cushion in the chair.

Oh, all you happy over the earth.
    That night, how could I sleep?
I lay and watched the lonely gloom;
    And watched the moonlight creep
From wall to basin, round the room.
    All night I could not sleep.

Rupert Brooke

YOU ARE GONE BUT YOU AREN'T GONE REALLY

I went swimming in the sea today
And laying down in my bed now, to go to sleep
I can still feel the motion of the waves

Simon Mole

BETWEEN THE COVERS

I sit soft on the sofa
with snow whipping my eyes,
with chill rock against my cheek.

Wolves howl,
but their tiny voices
vanish in the storm.

I need shelter,
to get under cover,
find a cave.

My cloak so thin,
my boots full of slush,
my eyes sting and my cheeks crackle.

I get up,
make a cup of tea,
look out the kitchen window at the summer.

A blackbird hops on the fence,
eyeing worms,
singing his snatch of sunlit song,

and then —
back to the sofa,
back to the mountain,
back to the winter,
back to the book.

A. F. Harrold

TALL NETTLES

Tall nettles cover up, as they have done
These many springs, the rusty harrow, the plough
Long worn out, and the roller made of stone;
Only the elm butt tops the nettles now.

This corner of the farmyard I like most:
As well as any bloom upon a flower
I like the dust on the nettles, never lost
Except to prove the sweetness of a shower.

Edward Thomas

BEST FRiENDS

You say this tree is a castle and I say OK
and we play and we climb for the rest of the day.

There's a spot down the garden where we talk for hours,
down with the snails and the foxes and flowers.

You say you've made a cake, would I like a slice?
I say OK and I pass you the knife.

I'm peeling an orange and I give you a piece
and you share your bag of your favourite sweets.

We're watching a scary film on the TV,
I can tell that you're frightened, say come sit with me.

When the moon's in the sky we chat under the covers.
We share our worries and we comfort each other.

You say you feel sad and you'd like to talk
so I cycle to yours and we go for a walk.

You make me laugh with that grin on your face.
The park with you is my favourite place.

In the arcade I lose and I don't get the prize
you put your coin in the slot and we play one more time.

You forget your sandwich, you're hungry at lunch.
So I split mine in two and we both have a munch.

I'm a red, you're a blue and your team wins the game
but I see the smile on your face, and it makes it OK.

The ice-cream man comes, but I don't have the cash
but you run to the van, you bring two lollies back.

Maths was never my strong point, I struggle with sums
but you show me how and you make it fun.

I wait for you after school so we can walk home.
When I'm with you, my best friend, I'm never alone.

Cecilia Knapp

FEBRUARY TWILIGHT

I stood beside a hill
Smooth with new-laid snow,
A single star looked out
From the cold evening glow.

There was no other creature
That saw what I could see —
I stood and watched the evening star
As long as it watched me.

Sara Teasdale

SNOW

Let the wild wind blow snow
Let the green grass grow snow
Let it always show snow
When they forecast the weather

Oh, that flitter-flutter flow snow
Oh, the gutter-glitter glow snow!
Of the Christmas long ago snow
Give us our merry measure!

And let us all go throw snow
In the tangled to and fro snow
In the frozen tingly-toe snow
Let us play together

And let's all shout 'HELLO SNOW
Hey, never ever go snow
We love you so' and, oh snow
Please shut the school forever!

Justin Coe

THE FOUR BEARS SPELL

(to keep you safe at night)*

Place Bertie Bear on the window sill
To guard against the giant dragons
Who roar past in the night
Breathing yellow fire

Place Big Ted at the door
To trip and lay low goblins
Who try to squeeze
Through the crack beneath

Place One-eyed Ted at the foot of your bed
To scare away the shadow monsters
Who hide in the darkness beneath you
And gurgle and groan

And finally
Keep Algy Bear beside you
To keep you safe and warm
From the cold breath of ghosts

*I've used my bears, but you must use your own.

Roger Stevens

THE DEAF MOUNTAIN

A mountain and a deaf mountain look the same.
But the deaf mountain can no longer talk to her
mountain friends.
Nor hear their stones of laughter tumbling down the slopes.
She can only gaze at them.

The deaf mountain thinks, '*This must be enough. This is all I have.*'

Sometimes a tear trickles down her face for the lost sounds.
The beat of the eagle's wings, the moan of the storm.
But her memories keep her strong.
On and on she stands alone among the other peaks.
The deer are kind and visit from time to time.
They understand why she never speaks.

A mountain and a deaf mountain look the same.
Both can see the clouds. Both can feel the rain.
But only one longs to hear the drum of it again.

Louise Greig

THE RiVER

The River's a wanderer.
A nomad, a tramp,
He doesn't choose one place
To set up his camp.

The River's a winder,
Through valley and hill
He twists and he turns,
He just cannot be still.

The River's a hoarder,
And he buries down deep
Those little treasures
That he wants to keep.

The River's a baby,
He gurgles and hums,
And sounds like he's happily
Sucking his thumbs.

The River's a singer,
As he dances along,
The countryside echoes
The notes of his song.

The River's a monster
Hungry and vexed,
He's gobbled up trees
And he'll swallow you next.

Valerie Bloom

BOOKWORM

A worm ate words. I thought that wonderfully
Strange — a miracle — when they told me a crawling
Insect had swallowed noble songs,
A night-time thief had stolen writing
So famous, so weighty. But the bug was foolish
Still, though its belly was full of thought.

Anon.

LiSTEN STARS,
EARTH TALKiNG

Adapted from a Native American song

listen stars moon sun and everything that moves in the
    heavens
a new life – human – has come into our midst
welcome it
make its path smooth so it can walk to my first hill

listen wind, clouds and rain and everything that circles
    round me
a new life – human – has come into our midst
welcome it
make its path smooth so it can run to the brow of my
    second hill

listen grasses, rivers, lakes, trees, mountains, and
    everything that lives here on me
a new life – human – has come into our midst
welcome it
make its path smooth so it can leap to the brow of my
    third hill

listen birds and all who fly in the air
a new life — human — has come into our midst
welcome it
make its path smooth so it can fly to the brow of my
    fourth hill

listen animals and all creatures who live in harmony
    with me
a new life — human — has come into our midst
welcome it
make its path smooth so it can travel far beyond all my
    hills

Zaro Weil

ABOUT THE AUTHOR

Matt Goodfellow is from Manchester. He spends his time writing and touring the UK and beyond visiting schools, libraries and festivals to deliver high-energy, inspirational poetry performances and workshops. Before embarking on his poetry career, Matt spent over 10 years as a primary school teacher. He is a National Poetry Day Ambassador.

ABOUT THE ILLUSTRATOR

Roxana de Rond is a freelance illustrator with a passion for drawing people and dogs. After years of moving between the States and the UK, she settled in Cambridge. In 2016 Roxana graduated with an MA in Children's Book Illustration at Anglia Ruskin University. Her book *Monty and Mortimer* was highly commended for the Macmillan prize and is now being published with Child's Play under the new name *Monty and Milo*.

ACKNOWLEDGEMENTS

The compiler and publisher would like to thank the following for permission to use their copyright material:

Abbott, Matt: 'Quinn' by Matt Abbott. Copyright © Matt Abbott. Used with permission of the author. With thanks to Quinn's family. **Awolola, Ruth:** 'Pockets' by Ruth Awolola. Copyright © Ruth Awolola. Used with permission of the author. **Bertulis, Debra:** 'Wild Horses of Hergest Ridge' by Debra Bertulis. Copyright © Debra Bertulis. Used with permission of the author. **Bloom, Valerie:** 'The River' by Valerie Bloom. Copyright © Valerie Bloom 2000 from *Let Me Touch the Sky* (Macmillan, 2000). Used by permission of Eddison Pearson Ltd. on behalf of Valerie Bloom. **Bromley, Carole**: 'Transition Day' by Carole Bromley. Copyright © Carole Bromley. Used with permission of the author. **Brownlee, Liz:** 'Chaffinch' by Liz Brownlee. Copyright ©Liz Brownlee. Used with permission of the author. **Carter, James:** 'Somewhere' and 'If You've Ever Seen a Wolf' by James Carter. Copyright © James Carter. Used with permission of the author. **Coe, Justin:** 'Snow' by Justin Coe. Copyright © Justin Coe. Used with permission of the author. **Coe, Mandy:** 'Black Bear Backs Up To The Giant Pine Tree' and 'The Superpower Song' by Mandy Coe. Copyright © Mandy Coe. Used with permission of the author. **Conlon, Dom:** '52 Blue – the loneliest whale' and 'Bee Buddies' by Dom Conlon. Copyright © Dom Conlon. Used with permission of the author. **Dean, Jan:** 'Earstorm' by Jan Dean. Copyright © Jan Dean. Used with permission of the author. **Gill, Nikita:** 'A Short List of Alternatives' by Nikita Gill. Copyright © Nikita Gill. Used with permission of David Higham on behalf of the author. **Greig, Louise:** 'To the Bears' and 'The Deaf Mountain' by Louise Greig. Copyright © Louise Greig. Used with permission of the author. **Hardy-Dawson, Sue:** 'Mother Tongue' and 'Letters from the Lost' by Sue Hardy-Dawson. Copyright © Sue Hardy-Dawson. Used with permission of the author. **Harrold, A. F.:** 'Between the covers' by A. F. Harrold. Copyright © A. F. Harrold. Used with permission of the author. **Kirtley, Sophie:** 'Wild Wild Girl' by Sophie Kirtley. Copyright © Sophie Kirtley 2022. Used with permission of the author. **Knapp, Cecilia:** 'Best Friends' by Cecilia Knapp. Copyright © Cecilia Knapp. Used with permission of the author. **Malik, Anjum:** 'Bloody Samosas' by Anjum Malik. Copyright © Anjum Malik. Used with permission of the author. **McLachlan, Dawn:** 'Half Term' and 'Don't Be Late' by Dawn McLachlan. Copyright © Dawn McLachlan. Used with permission of the author. **Mitton, Tony:** 'Window' by Tony Mitton. Copyright © Tony Mitton 2005, used with the permission of the author. **Mole, Simon:** 'You Are Gone But You Aren't Gone Really' by Simon Mole. Copyright © Simon Mole, 2022. Reproduced by kind permission of Simon Mole c/o Caroline